PR Rock Star
A Little Brand Book

Cyndy Hoenig

Celebrating stories.

www.BuzzBooksUSA.com

Copyright 2013 Cyndy Hoenig

Each author owns the copyright to his/her story.

Published by Buzz Books USA, an imprint of Athena Institute, LLC.

All rights reserved. No part of this book may be reproduced by any mechanical, photographic or electronic process or in the form of a phonographic recording; nor may it be stored in a retrieval system, transmitted, or otherwise be copied for public or private use except for "fair use" as attributed quotations in reviews of the stories or the book.

All characters in this book are fictional. Any likeness to persons or situations in the stories is entirely coincidental.

ISBN-10: 1938493095
ISBN-13:978-1-938493-09-6

Trade Paperback Edition

To schedule a speaking engagement or for publicity or bulk orders, email buzzbooksusa@me.com.

Table of Contents

Introduction...5

Chapter 1: pr rock star 101: What is PR and How Can It Help Me?...8

Chapter 2: get stage ready: Planning Your PR Strategy...14

Chapter 3: the custom concert poster: Finding the Angle & Delivering the Pitch...29

Chapter 4: the ticketmaster: The Media and Your List...40

Chapter 5: own the mic: Becoming an Expert & Problem Solving...46

Chapter 6: this is a live audience: Face Time & Being Human...52

Chapter 7: If you fall: Bad News & PR...56

Chapter 8: rock star manager: 10 Tips to Becoming Your Own Publicist...60

Chapter 9: backstage: Insider Tips & Tricks...65

Chapter 10: rock star tools: Templates to Go Forth and Publicize...78

Encore: social media tips I can't keep to myself...85

Encore two: list of 100 top business editors...93

Acknowledgements

To my friend and former boss **Larry Goldman** -- #1 Yankees Fan, Brilliant beyond Brilliant PR Strategist, and the man who took a chance on a girl who wanted an entertainment career with a very limited resume. Thanks Larry.

To my darling **Donald Draper** - Who taught me I could meet any goal as long as I was laughing, but who never seemed to get me to clean my coffee cups.

To **Shea Moseley** for all the typing -- and the patience.

To **Marc Grossman** and **Karin Olsen** - many thanks for your edits. I value your knowledge.

To **Shawn Blake** – who has the patience of a saint. You started my career in PR. You took me as her assistant, knowing that I knew nothing about PR, except that I wanted it. And, you taught me everything you know. Without her, I wouldn't have this career. Thanks, Shawnie.

To my publisher, editor, and really good friend, Malena Lott. Thank you so much for the idea for this book and especially for thinking I could write it. Without your gentle nudging, I would never have finished it. Here's to many more. Thank you so much.

To **Amy Freedman, Ashley Smith** and **Cynda Hoenig Thayer** for always believing in me.

To **Tyler, Austin, Katy, Maddie, Gunnar, Joseph, Chase and Ryder** – for giving me a reason to love life so much.

And, finally, to **Digger**, for keeping my feet warm as I wrote this book.

INTRODUCTION

In 1985 I packed up my car, the dog, and my four daughters, and headed for Los Angeles from my home in Oklahoma City. And along the way, married number three of four husbands. Well, at least he got me to L.A.

Seven years later, this husband left for greener pastures, in the form of a younger actress who he thought could help take him to new heights in the film industry. I applied for a job at a major PR agency on Olympic Boulevard, exaggerated my skills a bit and got the job. I was to be the assistant to a woman 10 years younger than me. Because of her and my boss, I learned the ropes. The *who, what, where, when, why* and *how* of public relations. I lived and breathed PR. I dreamed PR. I got to that office every morning at 6 a.m. to practice and study so I would be slightly more prepared by 8:30 a.m. when the office opened. The office opened and then magically, I got it, and it only took four months.

Over the next three years, I went from assistant to Director of the Television Division. It wasn't easy. During that time, I kept my ears wide open, listening intently so I wouldn't miss a thing. Eventually, I had my own accounts, responsible for developing publicity campaigns, devising creative pitching angles and aggressively pitching to both print and electronic media, maintaining talent relations, arranging and cover interviews, and creating collateral materials including press kits, press releases, presentations, proposals, status and clip reports, media alerts, releases and more. I developed strong relationships with the media, which contributed to my success in providing clients with exceptionally strong publicity coverage. As I said earlier, it wasn't easy, but it was well worth it. And, besides all this, I loved it. Every second of it. And the perks aren't bad either. Rubbing elbows with celebs, getting a good table at Spago, getting past the golden ropes at the newest "in" nightspot, and having those in the industry in-crowd acknowledge you at lunch at The Ivy.

I am passionate about public relations. It's thrilling and exhilarating and not easy at all. Making a simple strategic placement for a client is hard work and dedication. However, I have that unending drive. Oftentimes I find myself up half the night working furiously for a client. It's passion. It's heart. When the "magic" happens, it's victory, but short-lived because it's on to the next and the cycle continues. There is no normalcy in PR, which is a good thing I guess because I don't like normal; I like extraordinary.

The PR Diva has defined PR on her very popular blog as, "the ability to provide the answers before the public knows enough to ask the questions, or, we don't persuade people, we simply offer them reasons to persuade themselves." And, she's right. About this and a lot of other PR observations. Consider it more than simply a way to attract attention or influence people toward buying your product. PR is an art that creates an image of you and your business and presents it in a controlled, planned fashion that will convey exactly what you want to say without having to be obvious about it.

It is also the most overlooked marketing and sales tool, even though it's the least expensive, the least risky, the most effective, and the easiest to use -- when you understand how to use it. PR is the overall planning, approach, and strategy for dealing with the media, investors, stakeholders, clients, and potential clients. It is communication with your target market publicly. The bottom line is to get word out about you, your company, your products and services to those who could potentially buy from you. The good news about PR is the cost and the effectiveness when it's in front of your target market.

PR is also about human relations. It isn't merely getting your name in the paper or appearing on radio or TV. It's how you interact with and represent yourself to the world. PR begins as soon as you meet or are seen by others. It's about how you treat your clients, employees and suppliers. It's a full-time job that starts the moment you walk out your door each day - everything from how your phone is answered to how your staff presents themselves to what you're wearing that day.

With this book, you'll learn to think like a publicist. If you don't, you won't know what to do if something unexpected happens. You won't pitch the media in a persuasive way. You won't know who to call or what to write when an innovative campaign idea occurs to you.

CHAPTER 1
PR ROCK STAR 101
WHAT IS PR AND HOW CAN IT HELP ME?

I'm asked a lot of questions on a daily basis. Two are most important. The first is "What do you do exactly?" and the second is "What can PR do for me?" Let's take a look at the first one. What do I do exactly?

First, the role of the PR professional is to be the spokesperson and advocate for the brand, product, company, or firm, and ultimately help to keep an image that is favorable. We are the contact and relationship holder for the public as the title suggests. Keeping a favorable image does not, however, entail being dishonest or deceitful about the firm or company being represented. This position requires honesty, commitment, and integrity.

Some tasks that a public relations specialist may have to carry out, according to the gang at prmarketingcommunication.com, include:

- ✓ the writing of press releases, web content, and interview scripts
- ✓ being interviewed yourself by the media or
- ✓ other companies
- ✓ relaying the benefits of public relations to the rest of the company and its key stakeholders.

Without this sort of advocate for public relations, PR may not be viewed as an equally important company mix as advertising is, when in reality it is of equal or more importance than advertising, and can cost dramatically less. On top of that, we keep the rest of the company involved and up-to-date with the company's news, as well as what can be said if they are asked about a new product or rumor.

Furthermore, the public relations specialist will need to make constant correspondence with the media, including journalists, reporters, writers of blogs or websites, and people who manage podcasts or videocasts. This requires great communication and a very personable individual. It also requires patience, the ability to learn and listen, as well as common sense and conscientiousness.

And there's more:
1. Research. National research. Because I need to measure consumer awareness. Using this data, I can design a plan for my client.
2. Writing. All kinds of documents: fact sheets, news releases, media pitches, position papers, PowerPoint presentations, blog posts, web copy and more.
3. Plan special events. This gives me a vehicle for media coverage.
4. Manage crisis situations. To move the client past the crisis as painlessly as possible.
5. Talk to the media. This is why my relationships I have spent years cultivating with the media are so important. Critical, even.

6. Tell the truth. No matter what the temptation. I never chance undermining my credibility with my team, the client or employers.

7. Find advocates. I reach out and form alliances to be of help to the client.

8. Educate and continue to learn. I need to be one of the smartest people on the team. I am current on what's going on in the world, as well as the subject I am representing.

9. Use all the new media tools available. Everyone at my disposal.

Now for the second question:

"WHAT CAN PR DO FOR ME?"

1. PR builds your identity.
2. PR compels people to buy, invest, and do business with you.
3. PR generates name recognition.
4. PR gets your message across.
5. PR helps attract new clients. "People do business with people who they know, like and trust," my favorite quote about PR by the brilliant Jay Conrad Levinson.
6. PR increases your credibility. When people read about you, hear about you, or see you speaking, you are automatically considered an expert.
7. PR increases your visibility.
8. PR is very cost-effective compared to other marketing tactics. Just price advertising.
9. PR levels the playing field. Small businesses are made to appear larger than they are and this allows them to compete in any arena.

10. PR removes price objections. If people believe you're the best and only choice, they will pay your price.

Then social media comes along and changes the game. I love social media and I'm good at it. I have to admit that it took me several months before I completely "got" it, but it was well worth it. Social media is what PR needed to give back the charge, the thrill of the game. It's just another notch on the PR tool belt. Blending traditional and emerging technologies is just the ticket to boost the effects of PR.

As this chapter was titled "What can PR do for me?" I thought I would tell you what it's done for me: It has made me a well-known and well-respected PR person. I own my PR firm – Pure PR and I'm known throughout the world thanks to Twitter and Facebook where I have nearly 20,000 followers and friends. I know that's not a lot to Kim Kardashian or Lady GaGa but for a girl in the Midwest just trying to make a living, this is a good thing. And, I did it all without buying one ad. Because along the way, you have to remember to do a little PR on your own behalf, just as if you were the client.

PR Star Files

Suzanne Somers' Institute for the Effects of Addictions on the Family

In 1988, Somers wrote her autobiography, *Keeping Secrets* which was on the *New York Times* Best Seller List for 21 weeks. The book, relating her story of growing up as the child of an alcoholic became a Somers' trademark, although she herself does not drink, as it spurred discussions of the subject on a national level, and inspired her to start the *Institute* for the *Effects of Addictions on the Family*.

The opportunity was clear. Maximize coverage to raise awareness. Our approach included writing and distributing media kits nationwide; schedule a media tour to New York; hold a launch breakfast with Somers as the keynote; and a Speakers' Bureau for Somers to speak about what she knows best – how alcoholism affects the family.

Success came in the form of print coverage in the top 35 markets; and national press coverage in *People, Time, Newsweek, USA Today, Wall Street Journal, Parade, New York Times* and *Washington Post*.

The materials we prepared and distributed included the media kits containing Institute background information, bios of Somers and board members, and an in-depth Q&A.

A Little Brand doesn't have to be a celebrity to make an emotional appeal and create a professional campaign.

#PRTIP: Develop a low cost PR campaign and handle in house. PR is a powerful tool and a successful campaign lends credibility. To do PR in house, you need to be able to learn to write a press release, find the right contacts in the media to send it to and create a professional-looking press kit.

CHAPTER 2
Get stage ready
Planning Your PR Strategy

Most people think of PR as simply press coverage or publicity. It's so much more than that as you'll see in further chapters. In order to get press coverage, you must have news worthy of being covered. Unless you're a hot celeb, a scandalous CEO or have just created a cure for cancer, you're going to have to come up with the news angle, or story idea. Your goal needs to be to think like a reader, listener or viewer of the media. And, to understand just what news is.

News is all about the latest, greatest, biggest and most exciting things that are happening. News can be good and bad, and journalists are interested in both. If you have launched a new product, started a new service, moved offices, taken on more staff, just merged with a Fortune 500 company, lost a big order, are facing insolvency or just hit the jackpot, newspapers will be interested in talking to you.

News has two priorities: First, it must be current, and second, it must mean something to people. A story about the environment and a story about the Oscars can both be newsworthy, for different reasons.

News is new - it is new, first, never before, original, one-of-a-kind. It is information that we do not already know. You'll hear and see these words over and over in the news.

News is NOT what we already know.

There is an old saying in the news business that news is not "dog bites man". News is "man bites dog".

News is NOT ordinary.

News is timely - News is now. What is new and interesting did not happen last week or last month. It is going to happen soon, or it is happening now. We are a culture of instant information. We like to know what's going on now, live.

News is NOT what already happened.

Learning to think like a reader, listener or view of the media is key to a strategic and successful public relations plan or campaign. You have to ask yourself this question: Will the readers of this publication think this is interesting, entertaining, informative or useful? In other words, your story must stand out from the crowd.

Here's an example from an old friend and publicist, Michael Levine from his best selling book *Guerilla PR*: Candy Lightner, the founder of Mothers Against Drunk Driving, called a press conference to announce the forming of her organization after she lost her 14 year old daughter who was killed by a car driven by a drunk driver. Lightner appeared at the conference with her surviving daughter and sitting on the table in front of them were scores of beer cans. At the end of the conference, Lightner announced that each can of beer had been purchased by her underage daughter with an illegal ID. Her "Don't Drink and Drive message was brought home in a stark manner.

In planning a PR strategy, online and off, the goal is to get your friends and followers to become your brand evangelists and outperform your top sales performers by creating community around your brand.

1. Listen

A huge benefit in business is to jump on opportunities that others miss. The power of our digital world allows us in real time to find those opportunities. By creating alerts for ourselves, our products, our key players and competition, we know in real time who is talking about us and who needs us. Like the bat symbol for our business. If you don't have a listening strategy in place, you are missing the fundamental piece of the puzzle. Set alerts at Tweetbeep and Google.

2. Authenticity and Humanity

In every interaction you have with a customer— online or off. Be authentic. Authenticity is catnip to others, or haven't you heard? That's why reality TV is so popular right now. People want you to be real, authentic, and human. It's critical to your PR. Because PR is 80% cultivating relationships – with media, clients, prospects and friends. People want to buy from other people, from a trusted friend, not a logo.

3. Knowledgeable

Data is your friend and you want to cozy up to your market researchers and your IT folks to have a clear understanding of your customers. I don't just mean traditional data like visits and page views. I mean details. What social networks are they active on? What data are they sharing? Where are they getting their news? When you have that data, you have something powerful. Unlike traditional marketing where you spend and then you're stuck with the results, with social media and your online presence, you can monitor, tweak and alter in real time until you get it right.

4. Planning

Have a clear plan in place about your messaging. Your social network and online community is your real time focus group. Use them. But more importantly, make sure each spoke of your wheel has a communication plan in place to make sure each knows what is happening, and how each may work together to better the customer experience.

5. Honesty

I mean it. Practice it. If you screw up, own it. People always remember who screwed up. Save them the trouble, admit it, then explain how you're going to fix it. Think about all the disasters we've had in the past few years from financial institutes crashing to Senators on the Hill and golf pros hiding mistresses. The most effective way to build a trusting relationship with your customers is to be honest. The goal here is to combine your online and offline business know-how to create a customer experience where your customers become your best advocates.

Remember, when your customers know, like and trust you, they are giving you a shot, buying more and recommending you to others. How to accomplish this? Let us count the ways:

1. Share

The most effective weapon in your marketing arsenal is that handy "share" button. The stats behind the viral nature of our messages, that virtual endorsement by retweeting and liking is nearly impossible to put a dollar sign on. Consider every piece of content you create .... online and off. Is it shareable? From the email marketing pieces that go out to your customers to your blog posts, to your comments, are they shareable? Are your social networks included on all your collateral, business cards, letterhead, invoices, everything? Gone are the days of thinking one dimensionally .... everything you produce must contain your online info.

2. Encourage Feedback

Your customers want reviews; they want an "ask and answer". They want feedback. Make it available to them, and then take advantage of it. If you notice, more and more campaigns are including product testimonials. If you are scared to embrace Google reviews, Yelp or reviews that live on your own site, I have news for you.... you are setting yourself up for failure.

3. Identify Influencers

Every industry has them, every community has them. Find yours. This goes back to being knowledgeable -- you have to know your community.

Think about your influencers in three categories:
  a. those you can learn from
  b. those you can sell to
  c. those who can promote you.

Those you can learn from are those influencers where the information you obtain is helpful for your community. Those you can sell to are obvious, but you want those who will be your top sales performers. Finally, those who can promote you. These are the journalists, bloggers, and thought leaders who share with the world how fabulous you are.

4. Over deliver

It goes without saying, but under promise and over deliver. I mean not only in your service and the quality you offer, but how you engage with your customers and prospects. For example - over delivering means being a connector of people; identifying those within your community who would benefit from others within that community; promoting others; recognizing others…even acknowledging birthdays on Facebook. I have a feeling that some of you are already prepping your questions about ROI and wondering how a birthday wish is relevant to the bottom line of your business. Well, I have news for you. When it comes time to make a buying decision, who are those prospects going to remember? It's like this: He who has the relationship wins the client.

> **PR Star Files**

A Bank and *Race for the Cure*

The opportunity was to maximize exposure and media coverage for the Bank's presenting sponsorship of the Central Oklahoma Susan G. Komen Foundation's *Race for the Cure*.

Our approach: We developed media partnerships with KWTV-TV, *The Oklahoman*, Southwestern Publishing and Citadel Broadcasting. A comprehensive media kit was developed and disseminated to all local media outlets; Interviews with Bank representatives, survivors and family members were coordinated, and stories ran on KWTV and Citadel radio stations on a daily basis two weeks ahead of the race.

Capitalizing on the anticipation of the race, a special event was planned to kick of the festivities. "City in the Pink" was held two weeks out and resulted in two TV spots. We produced three PSA's, which ran continuously during the month of October. Press releases and media alerts helped maintain top-of-mind media awareness.

Success was realized in that the race was attended by almost 12,000 runners, an increase of 2,000 over the previous year, and was covered by our local CBS affiliate. Local DJ's from our radio media partner emceed the event with an anchor from our CBS affiliate. The extensive media relations campaign generated remarkable coverage with 6,610,824 impressions and $535,322 in cost equivalency.

A Little Brand can increase impact by creating partnerships to share the investment and grow the reach.

CREATING A SUCCESSFUL PR PLAN

1. Know your company's or client's current situation.
This is essential to knowing where the company now stands, what the company's market looks like, and what direction the company is headed.

2. Know your resources.
READ: budget, time and other resource limitations. This can help you better build your tactics and strategies considering the above resources.

3. Define Goals and Objectives
Also essential to the PR Plan having success, you must know where the company hopes to go. Like driving with no directions, a PR Plan with no goals or objectives. Is an aimless action with no knowledge of what could come, or even what results are expected. Be sure that the plan's objectives are in line with the rest of the company's overall objectives, and ensure that they are clear to all involved. A few examples might include: build goodwill, create or reinforce a brand, introduce a new product or service, generate sales or leads, establish yourself as an expert.

4. Determine target audience.
Your target audience refers to the kind of people you think are qualified to buy your products and services. This information is critical because you want to match your ideal client to the media that he/she reads, listens to or views. Once you do that, it's time to locate the journalists covering your beat.

5. Determine key messages and strategies.
Good communicators don't just wing it. They establish key messages, phrases of different lengths that provide a description of your company in understandable terms.

Develop your 10-second-elevator speech, a phrase that provides a description of your company in understandable terms in the time it takes to ride an elevator from the 2nd to the 10th floor. Here's mine: "I'm Cyndy Hoenig. I'm a PR Strategist and I make people famous."

6. Timeline
This needs to be realistic, but also challenging. Remember that there should be no lapses in the plan where press releases are being sent out, events are taking place, or media are being engaged. There needs to be constant reminders to the public that the company is alive and well, and that can be done with information being sent out consistently.

Develop a schedule -- your timetable, month-to-month, week-to-week, day-to-day.

7. Delegate obligations and responsibilities to your team to ensure all parts of the plan are completed. This action helps to ensure that everyone is on board and all have the same information so that the plan runs smoothly.

8. Develop your plan of attack. What communication vehicles will you use?
- Media Kit
- Press Releases
- Newsletter
- Blog
- Chamber of Commerce membership
- Community involvement
- Web site
- Facebook and Twitter
- Special events

9. Put measures in place to track the results of your campaign.
- Monitor online presence daily using @socialmention and Google alerts.
- Review results monthly. Make revisions when necessary.
- Find out what motivates your customers. How? Ask them.
- Suggestion area on website
- Clipping notebook
- Cost Equivalency & Impressions Report

10. Review the plan after implementation and conclusion. This should be the time when the team comes together and shares thoughts on what worked, what didn't and what could be done differently. This will ensure that future plans will be successful.

POLISHING AND POSITIONING

Your image needs polishing every so often or maybe it's time to create a new one. It's up to you. But, make sure it's exactly what you're trying to communicate. It's called branding and branding is about other people's perceptions of you. You have the power to control most of these perceptions with your actions and presentation.

Anybody out there remember the singer from Wales, Tom Jones? He sang hits such as: "It's Unusual," "What's New Pussycat?", "She's a Lady," and more. While building his career, his team came up with a brilliant beyond brilliant branding idea that would forever seal Jones' image as a sex symbol. But before I let you in on his strategy, you need to hear the backstory.

It was 1972 and Tom Jones was coming to Oklahoma City to perform a concert. I was able to secure two tickets on the floor, third row. And here he comes. His performance and style of dress (featuring his open, half-unbuttoned white shirt and skin tight black pants) were exactly what I had expected. He knew how to move those hips. The show was a panty-hurling frenzy of sexually charged adulation and good-time entertainment. READ: Women were throwing their panties on stage – all colors and sizes. And I was standing on my chair just itching to be part of that scene. I was so close. Had a hand on each side of my tiny white panties ready to yank, and something stopped me.

THANK GOD.

Years later, I went to work for a very famous PR man in Los Angeles – Jay Bernstein. We were having drinks at the Polo Lounge one evening and Tom came in and Jay introduced us. I told them my "Tom Jones and the panty story." When they finally stopped laughing, Bernstein and Jones filled me in on the publicity stunt that sent his career soaring. Bernstein was managing Jones in those days and before Jones had started playing Caesar's Palace, Bernstein paid 10 women $50 each to throw their underwear and hotel room keys on the stage. It caught on that very night and from then on, whenever Tom gave a concert, history repeated itself.

Polishing your image. Simply brilliant.

Positioning, along with branding and direct response, is one of your strategic communication tools. Positioning can be expressed in many ways, from a simple slogan to an entire campaign. Positioning, along with branding and direct response, is one of your strategic communication tools. "How you position your brand, product, or company might be the most important aspect of your marketing communications plan. Positioning can be expressed in many ways, from a simple slogan to an entire campaign. In most cases you should express it in every ad, perhaps as the tagline, and certainly in every editorial." *Source: AdCracker*

Positioning is that one descriptive sentence or slogan or image the brand is known for. It's that one specific idea that first comes to mind about the product. That one characteristic that sets the service apart from competitors.

Now, a little about **Personal Branding,** which I consider one of the most important parts of doing business. This can and should be done in any and every industry, whether you work at home or in an office. I think it's critical.

Personal Branding is the most potent tool for building a professional business that's ever been invented. A personal brand will help you do three things.
1. Turn your name into a distinctive product with very attractive qualities associated with it.
2. Attract a more profitable clientele.
3. Retain more top quality clients even when business is slow for everyone else.

You won't win business by talking about how much better you are than your competition, and you can't expect people to simply knock on your door and hand you their money. **Your only advantage is you.** What you do may not be unique, but you are. So instead of focusing on services or price, start to focus on you. Reach out to your target market and shape how clients, customers and prospects think about you and how they see you – so you can connect with them personally. That's what a personal brand does for you.

A brand also **promises a result and experience you can count on**. Your personal brand is the mental picture your prospects get when your name is mentioned. It represents your values, your personality, your expertise and the qualities that make you unique among your competitors. That's why it's so important to remain authentic to yourself as you create your brand.

Remember this: People want to work with and buy from people they know, like, and trust. Your brand is a promise. A promise that tells people what they can expect when they do business with you.

#PRTIP: Write a tagline that reflects who you are and what you do in the most precise way possible. Be able to deliver it in 10 seconds.

CHAPTER 3
The Custom Concert Poster
Finding the Angle & Delivering the Pitch

A great story idea gets attention. It can lead to promotions, awards and prestige for the people in the media. That's why the media angle is so important. It's also referred to as a news hook, news angle, or story idea, etc.

In order to get media coverage, you have to do something newsworthy. Your goal needs to be to think like a reader, listener or viewer of the media. What would interest you? Ask yourself this question: Will the readers of this publication think this is interesting, entertaining, informative or useful?

Self-interested, veiled attempts at promoting your business will fall flat. The media does not care about your company's success *unless their readers care about it*. The media does not care about your new product *unless you can help them understand how their readers are longing to know about the problems it solves*.

So, let's look at the following steps to help you get there:

1. Brainstorming

I love brainstorming. It's one of the most popular ways to find that perfect angle. Often others can see angles that you might have overlooked since you are so close to the subject. So, invite everyone in your office for a brainstorming session. Let everyone shout out ideas and don't veto any of them. No comments or judgments. Later, sort through the best ones and piggyback on others. Another hint: Brainstorm with the daily paper. Get into the habit of reading your paper with a notebook and pen in hand. Scan the headlines and ask yourself, what's in the news today that ties in with what I want to promote?"

2. *Listen to questions your customers ask of you.*
You might notice a trend starting. Or a really good idea for a story angle.

3. *What makes your business special?*
Don't just think of why it should be important but why it is special.

4. *What do you offer that is unique?*
Answering this question can help you find the angle. Consider the following list as it relates to you and your business:
- Product - Are you one of a kind, with unique features?
- Quality - Best ingredients, award-winning
- Service - Money back guarantee, two-hour delivery
    window
- Target Market - Dentists, young moms, high wealth individuals

- Style - Personal approach, will listen and design to your needs
- Price - Lowest price
- Selection - Largest selection in the southwest
- Location – convenience

5. What do you offer that competitors don't?
Remember, others may offer it, but it they don't promote it, you can promote AND claim it.

6. What do you offer that is so compelling, it drives people to act?
- One stop shop?
- Handle a wide range of services?
- Good location?

7. How will the reader's life be changed?
Leave the reader feeling the need to act on the information you present.

8. You must do something newsworthy.
You and your organization make news more often than you realize. You understand your biz more intimately than anyone, which gives you a better perspective on your market. The hurdle lies in your ability to recognize what makes a story and who the most appropriate journalists are to tell that story.

9. Read your trades.
What is the buzz in those trades? What are new developments in your field? Use your access to this

information to shape a story.

10. *Watch news and talk shows*. Comedians and late night talk show hosts have their fingers on the pulse of trends to which everyone can relate. Use them. Listen to them nightly.

11. *Work with the calendar*.
Have you noticed that weight-loss articles fill newspapers and magazines every January and tax tips abound in March? Editors have a pressing need for timely stories, but demand fresh twists that are relevant to their audiences.

12. *Work with holidays*.
Create a story angle by tying in with regular holidays or with a little-known but highly relevant holiday that you find in Chase's Directory of Events – chases.com. You can even make up your own special day and get publicity for it. Mayors will sometimes sign proclamations for these observances.

PR Star Files

Oklahoma City National Memorial 10th Anniversary

The opportunity: To manage and maximize exposure and media coverage for the OKC National Memorial's 10th Anniversary of the bombing of the Alfred P. Murrah Federal Building April 19, 2005.

Our approach: To ensure accurate and timely placements with print and electronic outlets, press releases were disseminated on a daily basis over a two-week period announcing the daily activities taking place. Executive interviews were coordinated with the executive director and chairman of the board of trustees to secure feature stories about the 10th anniversary commemorative plans in national and top-market newspapers, as well as key national radio and television outlets. Capitalizing on the anticipation for the event a press briefing was held two weeks before the actual day of the anniversary.

Success: The extensive media relations campaign generated over 500 media representatives attending, from national and international outlets. The wide-reaching coverage generated placements including CNN (Aaron Brown broadcast from the Memorial); NBC Nightly News (Brian Williams broadcast from the Memorial); ABC, CBS, FOX News, as well as local and regional coverage with all affiliates covering.

#PRTIP - Media angles must have some distinctive quality. Journalists sniff out what's different, not what's the same.

30 IDEAS FOR NEWSWORTHY MEDIA ANGLES

1. Announcement of an annual charity event/fund-raising activity
2. Business owner becoming involved in the local social component of community
3. Celebrity or sportsperson supporting the business
4. Changing and expanding employee structure to accommodate employee needs (job share, part time).
5. Creation of long-term relationship with local or well-known charity
6. Employee awarded special recognition in the community
7. Equal opportunity initiatives
8. Family-friendly initiatives
9. Flexible workplace arrangements (working from home)
10. High profile business person now employed by or advises the company
11. Humble beginnings to solid success story (rags to riches)
12. Increasing employee numbers due to business success
13. Launch of foundation arm of business
14. Market research led to a new business idea
15. New business to meet special market niche
16. New director appointed to board
17. New joint venture arranged

18. New service available
19. New strategic alliance developed
20. Offering annual award to a person or organization in the community
21. Offering unique leave program
22. Official launch of a new business
23. Personal hobby became a business
24. Personal story as the inspiration behind a business start-up
25. Research and development findings and product developments
26. Social contributions to the local community
27. Speaker at a public or industry event
28. Sponsoring employees for further education
29. Sponsorship of an event or person
30. Staff retention and engagement initiatives

The Pitching Process

The pitching process is 98% preparation and 2% execution. This is critical and what truly leads to successful media placements. Before you make that all important pitch, you must first tackle a few tasks: I've broken it down into 10 steps.

1. Find your target audience. What media do they read, listen to, and view? These types of media are your target media outlets. Ask yourself: "Who will be interested in this story? Which outlets will reach these people?" Start your media list. This list should include:

- ✓ Local daily newspaper
- ✓ Weekly newspaper
- ✓ Business journal
- ✓ Trade publications covering your type of business or expertise
- ✓ Local radio and TV
- ✓ If it's a product or service that can be sold outside of your community, include national press as well.

2. Find the journalist, editor or producer covering your beat. These will be available on the outlet's website. Research the reporter. Read his past stories and check out contact preferences. We're going to talk about your media list in the next chapter.

3. Research the media outlet to make sure it is a good fit for your story idea. Familiarize yourself with the outlet and its particular focus or personality.

4. Write your press release. Your release needs to be directly important to the audience. People don't care what a shovel is made of, or whether or not it has a wooden handle. They care about the hole it can dig. Sell the hole.

5. Most releases are delivered via email. Do not send an attachment without permission.

6. Prepare Pitch Points with all the pertinent facts about your company and the story you're pitching before you call or email.

7. Prepare more than one story angle. Don't waste everyone's time by putting all of your PR eggs in one basket. Have a few angles to toss out.

8. Call your contact with a brief pitch. Your first four words should be, Are you on deadline? Once you get the contact on the phone, explain why you think the story is important. In 20 seconds or less.

9. Give the journalist or producer the heads up that you'll be sending a release and ask for permission to send an attachment, if you have one, and you probably will. The release, a photo, perhaps a bio, etc.

10. Follow up in a couple of days to make sure said

reporter received your release and if additional information is needed.

> **PR Star Files**

I remember a pitch I made to one of the editors of *TV Guide*. I was handling a show called *Fortune Hunter* that ran on FOX in the early 90s. It wasn't doing well in the ratings and the producers were desperate to save it. I was definitely feeling the pressure. So, I called one of the editors at *TV Guide* and pitched a story. I think the pitch was the James Bond type gadgets used in the series. And, this is what this editor said to me: "If that piece of trash is still on the air in six weeks, I'll give you a cover story!" Obviously, *TV Guide* didn't like the show either. So, what could I do? I laughed and thanked him, and told him we would do everything we could to keep it on the air long enough to warrant that story. Well, it didn't last, so I had to call him back and eat crow. But, guess what? It bonded us as friends. Even though the pitch didn't go anywhere, it was huge for the relationship. It went with me the entire length of my television career in Los Angeles. And thanks, Mr. Editor at *TV Guide*, you know who you are.]

#PRTIP: HARO (Help A Reporter Out) -- http://www.haro.com. A must when doing your own PR. HARO is a free service that connects journalists with expert sources. There are three emails a day that include reporter queries that you can respond to if you are a fit for their story.

CHAPTER 4
THE TICKETMASTERS:
THE MEDIA AND YOUR LIST

It's never too soon to start building your media list. A media list is always a work in progress; it's never a finished product. You'll be adding and updating on a weekly, if not daily basis. Always carry something with you to record information. But first you have to find your target audience, or target market.

To find your target market, think about the demographics of your ideal client: age, gender, income, geography, etc. For example, if you own a pizza place in Norman, OK, your target audience might be college students, young singles and young families in Norman. If you're a business consultant, your target audience might be Fortune 500 companies in the United States and large companies throughout the world. The more specific you are, the better you will be able to tailor your public relations efforts to the right audience. Who do you want buying from you?

Now you need to match your ideal client to the media that he/she reads, listens to or views. This will take a little research on your part. The media list might include daily and community newspapers, business journals, Chamber newsletters, radio stations, TV stations, local magazines, and national media outlets.

Organize your media list into a spreadsheet

including the following:

    Media Outlet
    Contact Name
    Title
    Email Address
    Phone
    Fax
    Mailing address
    What they cover

A Few Sites to Help You Find the Right Fit:

1. LinkedIn Search -- http://www.linkedin.com. With LinkedIn's search feature, you can find specific contacts that fit your criteria. You can search using the term journalists within a 50-mile radius of your zip and you'll see hundreds of thousands of contacts.

2. Internet Public Library -- http://www.ipl.org/div/news. A searchable newspaper directory of popular magazines and newspapers organized by their respective subject area or geographic focus. Each individual listing includes a brief description of the outlet's coverage area, along with a link to their website.

3. Yahoo! -- http://www.dir.yahoo.com/news_and_media. Here you can browse newspapers, magazines, radio and

TV, and other news sources by subject, type and region.

4. U.S. Newspaper List -- http://www.usnpl.com. Links to newspapers and TV.

5. Newspapers Worldwide -- http://www.refdesk.com/paper.html. Another comprehensive listing of world newspapers.

6. NewsLink -- http://www.newslink.org. Offers links to U.S. and foreign newspapers, magazines, radio and TV.

7. TradePub -- http://www.tradepub.com. Works with business and trade magazine publishers to market free subscriptions to qualified professionals. This is your one-stop-shop for subscribing to a wide-range of free business and trade publications of interest to you. It's also a great place to find outlets you'll want to add to your media list.

And don't forget BLOGGERS.

1. Regator -- http://www.regator.com. This site posts the best blog posts. Good for finding the most relevant posts on whatever subject related to your biz.

2. Technorati -- http://www.technorati.com. A blog search engine. You can use it to search for blog posts on any subject.

3. Alltop -- http://www.alltop.com. You'll find all the top blogs on any particular subject you're looking for. This helps you identify bloggers and to keep up with current trends in your industry.

4. You will also want to connect with journalists, editors and producers on Twitter. Start following those who cover in your industry so they will get to know you. Find them at: muckrack.com and twitteringjournslists.pbworks.com

You can build the list yourself, or purchase one of these:
FinderBinder.com
MediaFinder.com
Vocus.com
Cision.com
EasyMediaList.com

Always contact the reporter/writer/editor who deals specifically with what your press release, advisory, pitch, etc. talks about. And, do your homework. Read his or her last five articles. Journalists hate when you call to make a pitch and you don't know what they cover.

None of these resources will provide anywhere near the volume or accuracy of information found in commercial media databases like Vocus or Cision. It's true that you get what you pay for when it comes to media research.

And while you're at it, you also want to learn how the media works. Know who your target outlet services, deadlines, when they publish or air, and their current trend for stories. Add all this info to your database.

When I read or watch the news, I'm looking for possibilities, guest editorials, trends to tie in to, or talk shows that might book my clients. I look at websites to determine what editorial calendars look like for the year and news programs to get a feel for the angles of the day. You never know when an idea might hit you and you want to be ready to pitch. And, while we're on the subject of pitching, hear this: Do not be afraid to pitch. You pitch your business, company, products and services on a daily basis. The media is no different. They need people to pitch their ideas. They can't think up all those stories on their own. Don't worry. You'll get over the nervousness of pitching after just a few calls.

In everything I do, I look for opportunities. Which reminds me of a Suzanne Somers story. We were on the set of "Talk Soup" which today is called "The Soup" on the *E Channel*. The producers always asked Suzanne to guest host when the host was on vacation. She loved the guest spot, except that we had to tape it at 6 a.m. daily for a week. During the time we were publicizing the ButtMaster, we were once again hosting. Suzanne was having a ball with the hosting duties and showing off the ButtMaster. At one point we went to commercial and she was fooling around with the BM by putting it there her head. I told her to leave it on when we came back from commercial, which she did, and she read her next few lines with that contraption propped on top of her blonde hair. The following Monday on the cover of the Life & Arts section of the *New York Times*, was a picture of Suzanne taken directly from the "Talk Soup" episode with the BM on her head. The cutline read: "What won't Suzanne Somers do to sell her products?" We couldn't have afforded that level of publicity. It was golden. By the way, nine million ButtMasters were sold that year. Not bad.

#PRTIP: Make a list of your best clients. What media outlets do they follow? Find out. This starts your media list.

CHAPTER 5
OWN THE MIC:
BECOMING AN EXPERT & PROBLEM SOLVING

One of the best lead generators is the free publicity generated when you are perceived to be a recognized expert in your industry. It doesn't matter what field of business you are in. If your clients and the media perceive you to be an expert, they will seek you out for advice, your perspective on stories they are researching or even to offer you business.

In order to be an expert, you must study your subject thoroughly. It is said that with a 1,000 hours of practice you become an expert. Most of us work around 2,000 hours per year, so you can see it doesn't take long to acquire the knowledge you need. If you have been working on your specialty for a while, you are already an expert. Your job is to become known as an expert.

TIPS TO ESTABLISH YOUR EXPERT CREDENTIALS

1. Figure out your uniqueness. And develop it into your slogan. Use those phrases everywhere, on Facebook, Twitter, in your elevator speech. It should be just a few words or a line and put it everywhere -- from your business cards to your website.

2. Give face time. Make sure people know and see your photo. Do you have an "official" current photo? Have you plastered it as many places as possible? You are the brand: People have to know who you are.

3. Make a list of your best 20 revenue customers. Then, figure out which media outlets they follow. Make up a list of the 20 editors or journalists that most influence your 20 clients. Create a media tip list for those 20 journalists and on an irregular basis, only when you have ideas or things you know they want, send it to them.

4. Don't just donate time, stake out a leadership position. At an association that can benefit from your participation where you'll meet and help others.

5. Be seen and network. With clients, current, former and prospective. Attend at least one function per week. You never know who you'll meet and who will hire you. I attended a club meeting several years ago that I had tried to get out of. I almost played sick. I went anyway. A very attractive young woman sat across from me and overheard me telling someone what I do for a living. The attractive woman sitting across from me? She was the director of communications at a medium-size hospital and she was looking for a PR team. I got the account. I was in the right place at the right time. If I hadn't attended that meeting ... well, let's just say that the account would have gone to some other firm. She wouldn't have known about me.

6. Speaking Engagements. You've bottled a lot of information and experience over the years. Are you repackaging it? Turn those ideas into an e-book. What are you selling? Solutions, ideas, driving lessons or therapy? If you have a book, it will start conversations that end in conversions and business for you.

8. *Have testimonials available and use them.* What do people say about you on the street? Find out by asking around.

PROBLEM SOLVING

If you will become a problem solver, you will also establish a relationship between you and a client that is hard to break. You will also make yourself invaluable to clients, and prospects will be running to you.

Create ideas. You'll become the go-to expert in your particular industry. Publish your ideas and solutions on your website, on Facebook, tweet them, blog about them. Send them to appropriate journalists. The news media today is everyone who can find you on the Internet. Publish your info and ideas for people to find when they're searching for answers to their problems. Here's the thing: people know their problems. They don't know your solutions. The blogs, comments, and news releases you publish reach the media, your competitors, and your buyers who are searching the Internet.

Here's a good example of problem solving. Again, a ButtMaster story. I was publicizing the ButtMaster, and

I wanted the cover of *People* magazine. It was a difficult pitch as most journalists and TV producers saw it as an advertisement. All of a sudden, I got a pretty good idea. I staged a photo shoot in Suzanne Somers' assistant's pool. I had her favorite photographer and her hair and makeup people. She wore a leopard print bathing suit that she had bought in St. Tropez 16 years earlier, and we had her floating on a beautiful pink tube in the water. She looked great and not at all 49, which was her age at the time. So, back to *People*. With photo in hand, I pitched People using the age angle. At 49, Suzanne Somers looked fantastic, at least 12 years younger. Here is what I pitched: "Remember Aunt Bea on the old Andy Griffith Shows? Well, she was playing a 50-year-old woman. And the Golden Girls were playing 55-year-old-women. And, I produced the photos of Suzanne in the leopard bathing suit. I rest my case." They agreed and lose bought it and the cover ran on January 27, 1996.

PR Star Files

University of Phoenix National Baby Showers

Out of 50,000 babies born in Oklahoma yearly, one-third are born into poverty. The baby showers are an effort to secure baby items to be donated to Department of Human Services and distributed to newborns. Our task was to manage exposure and media coverage.

We approached prominent women in Oklahoma City, inviting them to host private baby showers in their homes, including Oklahoma's First Lady, Kim Henry. The University of Phoenix hosted a hostess luncheon, which became a great photo op for our media partner *Friday* newspaper. Our local theme park, Frontier City agreed to host the state's largest baby shower at the park. Each person who bought a baby gift received half off their price of admission. Press releases and media alerts on the public showers were sent out to all Oklahoma media in an effort to create interest from photographers, print publications and broadcast outlets. Our radio partner, Citadel network provided a remote at Frontier City, which drove traffic to the park. We secured media partners in Citadel Communications, Frontier City, Ideal Homes and *Friday* newspaper. Coverage was received in all major Oklahoma City media, and donations well exceeded 10 times as much as the previous year – thousands of baby items filled three semi-trailer trucks.

#PRTIP: Good PR is generated when you're perceived as an expert in your industry. Write an E-book, blog, comment, tweet.

CHAPTER 6

THIS IS A LIVE AUDIENCE:
FACE TIME & BEING HUMAN

Face Time is very simple, and we're not talking about the Apple product. It's meeting in person. With social media reigning as the ultimate communication tool, Face Time gets kicked aside. But read on and you'll understand why Face Time matters *even more* now.

Face Time builds trust and relationships. Trust leads to happy customers. Happy customers leads to returning customers, which leads to word of mouth customers, which leads to more customers. Take your customers and prospects to lunch or dinner. You'll be able to learn how you can better serve them and get to know them on a personal level. And pick up the check. Always. People won't remember what they had to eat but they will always remember who picked up the check. You'll be recognized as someone they know and like and that translates trust. You're probably wondering why this matters? He who has the relationship wins. As in clients and customers. Every time.

Why it Matters: Being Human

In every interaction you have with a client -- online or off, be human. It's why editors love the human story and why we all love to hear, "have a great day." Being human also means forgetting the marketing speak and choosing to connect with clients and customers in the language they use to find you. Forget that salesy copy. Create relationships. This also means putting a face and a voice on your brand online. For example, on your blog, show your personality, your fun and your passion through your writing. If the human experience weren't so important, "Tweet-ups" and "Meet-ups" wouldn't be so popular. Or drinks after work, lunch dates and coffee meetings.

Remember the film "Castaway" with Tom Hanks? This film was written by Bill Broyles from Austin, Texas. I had an interesting conversation with him once at a restaurant in Austin. When Bill was approached to write the screenplay, the studio sent him to a deserted island for a week to get a feel for how Hanks' character might feel while alone on the island for four years before being rescued. Broyles told me that the worst thing he experienced was not having any human connection. And he was there for only a week. That's when and why he decided to create the character of "Wilson," the soccer ball.

Why it Matters – Leadership

Leadership in your community will go a long way and to an organization, stake out a leadership position. You'll meet and help others, as well as showing off your talents. Leadership in your community will go a long as you meet and work with other, as well as showing off your talents. You will piggyback on the positive PR these organizations garner. A very good thing.

About a year ago, I was pitching a company in Oklahoma City for their PR and Social Media accounts. During the pitch, the president of the company asked me why another company of the same kind got all the print and TV coverage. Well, listen to this. It just so happened that the head of the competition was on several community boards, went out a minimum of three times a week to dinners and events, and socialized with everyone there, it's also called networking. Therefore, all the attention and most of the business went to him. So, how did we fix this you ask? We designed a PR strategy that included charitable giving, community relations and media relations with a heavy dose of active involvement with a couple the client's favorite charities. It took time, but it worked, slowly at first, but then just fell in line. We gave the competition a good run for their money.

PR Star Files

Boutique Law Firm

Our opportunity was to increase visibility in Oklahoma's legal and business markets. We implemented a comprehensive PR plan; attracted media attention though story ideas; positioned the law firm partners as expert spokespeople; obtained speaking engagements; and created memorable marketing materials.

We pitched each of the 77 Chambers of Commerce in the state of Oklahoma regarding a complimentary speaking engagement by one of the attorneys. Our attorneys spoke to exactly half of these Chambers and new clients were found in each market.

We looked deep for stories. One story was the launch of a legal novel that one of the partners wrote. We prepared a huge PR campaign around this launch and received feature stories in all three major newspapers in the market. Another partner has a map collection at his home. We pitched a story on what attorneys do in their spare time. This story was interesting because the partner has maps from the 1200's to the present. The story was two full pages in the business section of the daily newspaper.

Marketing materials created included media kits, which were made downloadable on their web site. Hard copies were also created and left in the lobby of the firm, as well as traveling along with the attorneys in their cars. They each kept a few with them should they encounter prospects.

The resulting body of work – articles, media quotes, profiles, speaking engagements, etc. – delivered third-party validation and showcased the law firm's work and expertise. Distributing reprints and eprints, posting on the website and Facebook and more, extended visibility, as well as the shelf life of the PR investment.

#PRTIP: Customers have choices and if you're not consistently vying for their attention, you'll fall off their radar screens.

CHAPTER 7
IF YOU FALL
BAD NEWS AND PR

How you handle the bad news will play a large role in how your good news will be met by the media in the future.

Not having the right processes in place to pre-empt or deal with a crisis can easily turn a minor situation into a full-scale disaster. Corporate reputation is a delicate thing, with even the slightest tarnish affecting customer and stakeholder perception, sales and share price.

But how can you protect that reputation and, if the worst happens, defend it?

Prevention is better than the cure.

First, it is crucial you have a communications policy that includes a process for tracking and responding to market issues effectively. A crisis can often be averted if you anticipate what's happening out there, rather than being forced to react to it.

As the cause of an immediate crisis is often due to activity within the company, the policy should include a system for ensuring that the communications department and their agencies are quickly apprised of any developments such as redundancy, client losses, or acquisitions. This will ensure everyone is communicating the same, up to date information.

Taking control of a crisis

Whatever the scale and type of the crisis, you need to own it from the start. This is essential as, although it's very rare that you can change negative opinion, you can contain and minimize it if you take control early on.

By tracking market issues, you can become part of the debate from the start and hopefully defuse the situation. As public interest builds, you can have an impact on the evolution of an issue and maintain control. The media will often influence the development or death of an issue so it is essential to use it to make sure your view is heard.

A question and answer document setting out the company stance and providing strict guidelines for comment will ensure that one single and consistent message is communicated. Make sure spokespeople use the statements and stick to the agenda, so they cannot be pressured by a journalist.

While it is imperative that you acknowledge a crisis situation as quickly as possible, keep statements factual and succinct, saying why the situation has arisen and what is being done about it.

Honesty is the best policy and appearing to be open will keep the media on your side. If you don't talk to them they will become hostile, so communicate regularly to update them either with statements or press conferences. Never refuse to do an interview and never admit liability or speculate.

Keep it simple

Understand what motivates the aggrieved and respond empathetically, answering all their concerns. A heavy-handed response won't buy you any friends, which you need in a crisis. Keep responses simple so they are easy to understand and there is no chance of them being misunderstood. Don't dilute your point by losing focus - keep to no more than three key messages to ensure your position is communicated correctly by the media and understood by your market.

To protect your reputation in the future, always evaluate the result you intended against the actual outcome of a crisis. Reviewing the entire process will strengthen it and contain any future situations. How to protect your company reputation during a crisis. (n.d.). Retrieved from http://www.bytestart.co.uk/how-to-protect-your-company-reputation-during-a-crisis.html

Crisis Checklist:

- ✓ Are you prepared with facts and figures so you can respond to a crisis quickly?
- ✓ Have you written down lists of leading, difficult, tricky and nasty questions that could be asked of you in a controversial situation?
- ✓ Do you have the answers to them?
- ✓ Discuss your answers with your lawyer.
- ✓ Never say "No Comment." It's like pleading the 5th.
- ✓ Practice these questions and answers with your spokesperson.
- ✓ Do not restate misconceptions and wrong

information.
- ✓ Respond promptly.
- ✓ If you don't know the answer, say so.

#PRTIP: Bad PR? Respond immediately and never lie. The media are trained to investigate and they WILL find the truth. Just ask Tiger Woods, Bill Clinton, or any member of Congress.

CHAPTER 8
Rock star manager
10 steps to becoming your own publicist

1. Define your mission
What is your biz about?
What are the objectives?
Who is your target audience?

2. Study the media.
Learn how the media works. Be aware of who your target outlet serves, what their deadlines are, when they publish or air, and their as well as their current trend for stories.

3. What makes your story different?
Not all media outlets are appropriate for every type of business.

4. Be prepared for the opportunity.
Create a press release, consisting of: release announcing your company or product your story, aka backgrounder; a headshot on a disc, fact sheet; bio; contact info.

5. Think with a plan.
Identify what you want to promote, your target

audience you want to reach, tools you'll need and media vehicles to get there.

6. *Promote yourself.*
Brand yourself. You are an expert in your field. Execute your plan via speaking engagements, volunteering and becoming a true member of your community. Write an editorial or op-ed column, blog and network. I know it's difficult to sing your own praises, but if you don't do it, who will? But, remember this: Be humble. Always ask the question, "What can I do for you?" And listen. Trust me, the person you're networking with will eventually get around to you. And, you will appear much more appealing as a business resource, without the stigma of exhibiting that annoying self-absorbed behavior.

7. *Polish your image.*
What is the perception of your image? Ask friends and family what impression they have of you.

8. *Secure a mentor.*
Be clear with expectations and time and make it a two-way street. What do you have to offer? Then, become a mentor to someone else.

9. *Create and maintain key relationships.*
Identify people with common interests and different skills. Be a good friend and stand by your word.

10. *Empower your life.*
Give to your community. A great deal of business is done while volunteering, which can provide you a legitimate aura of leadership, credibility, dedication and commitment. Expand your base of key contacts. Become a board member and create a positive perception of who you are.

Bonus tip: *Honor your process and believe your own publicity.*
You are the best salesperson you have. PR is about knowing your work and not underselling yourself to secure and/or maintain business. Position yourself as an expert now. Editors, producers, bookers, publishers and online outlets are looking for original, inspiring and creative stories to capture each hour, day, week and month.

PR Star Files

The Crew
The Crew was a half-hour comedy, focusing on the lives of four 20-somethings working together as flight attendants and living in South Beach. The cast included Jess Jameson, played by Rose Jackson, who was born and raised in Philadelphia with a tell-it-like-it-is attitude; Maggie Reynolds, played by Kristin Bauer, a ultra-conservative girl from Salt Lake City; Randy Anderson, played by Charles Esten, a handsome good ol' Southern boy who became a flight attendant to meet women; and Paul Steadman, played by David Burke, a warm, and

utterly charming guy who dreams of finding love and settling down, if only he could find the right man. Jamie Wooten (The Golden Girls, Golden Palace) and Marc Cherry (Desperate Housewives) were the executive producers.

My job? To prepare and provide a high-profile publicity campaign that will launch this series into the top 15 of the Nielsen Ratings. After preparing all the necessary media materials (press kit, photos, announcement release, bios, Q&A's, and production notes), I devised a plan that I thought was brilliant beyond brilliant: I would get a plane, a real one with real pilots and flight attendants, to travel with our cast and crew to the airline's hub and have their professional crew members give our cast a few lessons on how to do it right.

So, next step – Southwest Airlines and *Entertainment Tonight*. I wrote a pitch letter to the folks at SW at the Los Angeles base and they gave us a resounding "YES!" Next, I pitched *ET* and offered them an exclusive to tape this segment for an upcoming program and they enthusiastically came on board. Rose Jackson, Kristin Bauer, Charles Esten and David Burke plus the crew of *The Crew* boarded our SW flight at 8 a.m. on a Friday morning at LAX. Our cast was literally taken under the wing (pardon the pun, but I thought it was clever.) of three experienced SW flight attendants for a day of on the job training.

We took a flight from LAX to Oakland for a bit of flight attendant training before the cast would tackle their comedic roles on the series. En route to Oakland, the four actors were able to observe first hand just how the pros do their jobs. Once the plane landed in Oakland, they were transferred to the airline's flight base and were officially trained by the SW flight attendants at their in-flight training center, which included demonstrations inside the flight simulator. Jackson, Bauer, Esten and Burke had the opportunity to practice their newly-honed craft on board the return flight to LAX, where they served the passengers drinks, passed out peanuts, doled out pillows and blankets and even announced the safety tips over the P.A. system.

Needless to say, all on board had an unforgettable flight. The segment aired on *Entertainment Tonight* a few weeks later as part of their Fall Series Special and was deemed a huge success. The moral to this story is this: Always think big. No matter what size your business is, always think big.

#PRTIP: Big mistake - People think PR works faster than it does. Don't give up on a PR campaign if you don't get immediate results. Remember, PR is a marathon, not a sprint.

CHAPTER 9
BACKSTAGE
INSIDER TIPS & TRICKS

To say I've lived and learned is an understatement. Why not make the most of my blunders and blockbusters? A few of my favorites I've developed over the years.

PR GUIDELINES

1. When the media calls, stop what you're doing and give them your full attention, remembering that these are relationships that you're building.

2. You have control over advertising; you have minimal control over PR. A media piece may not contain the story you had in mind. It may focus on a different angle. The reporter determines what angle to use, depending on his/her needs and information you provide. You may not like a quote that was attributed to you, or you may not like how you looked on TV. This is part of the PR process.

3. Sometimes, after a phone interview, you will be misquoted. This is pretty typical. Unless it is truly a libelous or slanderous comment, you should take it in stride. DO NOT decide to complain to the reporter, or you will certainly not be getting any press, at least not favorable press, in that media again. Sure, you prefer a feature story about your business. However, even a brief mention can be very valuable to your publicity goals. Most media outlets work on many more stories that cover trends or groups of businesses in an industry, instead of profiling just one business. You can be scheduled for an interview, and it may get cancelled at the last minute due to another news story that takes priority. This is typical in the media and something you should understand.

4. *Do not discuss other media coverage unless you are specifically asked*. The media overwhelmingly prefers to report stories and use sources that are not overexposed. Bringing up other media you have been covered in is at best a turnoff, and at worst will result in the reporter deciding not to cover your story.

5. *Give several contact numbers to your interviewer*. The press waits for no one.

6. *Be realistic about when the media will cover you*. Typically, daily newspapers, radio and TV have a one-day to three-month coverage window. Magazines have a two – three-month to one-year window. The lead times vary depending on editorial calendars, seasonal coverage and breaking news.

7. *The media chooses when they want to run a story; you have little control over when they run it, unless it is tied to a timely event.* While you would love to see yourself or your organization on the 6 p.m. news or the front-page of the business section, the media may have other stories slotted for those options, or they may need to fill a space in another segment.

8. *And then there's Breaking News...*
And this kind of news takes precedence over everything else.

BASICS OF GOOD MEDIA RELATIONS

- ✓ Is your personal pitch prepared so you can be brief and to the point?
- ✓ When you call, what are the first four words you'll use? "Are you on deadline?" Very important.
- ✓ Leave a maximum of two messages. Then call until your party picks up.
- ✓ More than one story angle ready?
- ✓ Have press materials ready to be emailed at a moment's notice. Do they include backgrounder, links with exact addresses, quotes, bios, photos on disc.
- ✓ Never go "off the record." If you don't want it published, don't say it. Every thing you say is on the record, if it's said to a reporter. Don't take any chances, even if it's a friend. That goes double for social media, it's like a photo, it's forever out there.
- ✓ Be prepared to gracefully accept 'no.'

- ✓ Do you know the deadlines? Lead times?
- ✓ When making follow-up calls, do you have additional facts or pitch points to tempt journalists to cover your story?
- ✓ Have you recorded all into your follow-up sheet?

Tips to Increase Name Recognition

1. Bring your **image and message** under a brand. Develop all collateral and image materials (web, stationery, logo, tagline, mission statement, cards, postcards, brochures, elevator pitch, newsletters, letters, project sheets, resumes, bios, firm description, etc.) to coincide with the brand and your message.

2. Develop a **mission statement** that shows your reason for being and the value you provide to your customers.

3. Develop a **memorable tagline** that expresses who you are and what you do.

4. Make a **matrix** of all those you'd like to reach in the next year and the potential influencers on those people. Develop a timetable and calendar of outreach.

5. Regularly **write and pitch feature story ideas** to the media.

6. **Diversify** all marketing, PR and media to reach the markets where your clients are to be found (as opposed to marketing within your own service industry).

7. **Participate** (attend, speak, host, present, show) in at least two national and local **industry conferences per year.**

8. Get known for **niche expertise** or specific industry knowledge. (speak, write, present, teach).

9. Participate and **sponsor local charitable efforts**; get your name in the program the charitable cause distributes; get your name in the press surrounding the event.

10. Develop a **calendar** of local and regional events in your locale and make your company visible in the areas most related to your company and your potential clients' interests.

11. Post your calendar of **appearances** and participation on your website.

12. Plan a **media release** before and after each event.

13. Hire an **industry professional** to conduct a survey on your behalf; post the results on your website. Publicize the results most important to your industry.

14. Establish your brand by regularly updating the **financial value** or potential value associated with your brand. Quantify results achieved and

add these results to your brand value. Communicate through all methods, the value of your brand to those associated with it.

Branding your company is key to influencing a memorable response in the minds of your chosen audience. It is not only the name recognition of your firm, but also the perceived value of your organization. Capture these essential branding elements and begin to cement a positive branded image for your business.

Ready to tackle your PR plan, but not sure what you have to say? Brainstorm using these 30 reasons you may have sending a press release the media will pay attention to.

> **PR Star Files**

A Very Famous Blonde Actress with a Hit TV Show

This actress was making $500,000 per episode on her sitcom that was in its seventh season. She was a handful. But particularly difficult during this season. I swear she was going through menopause. In fact, just to show you what we were up against, here's a good story. We were all at a table read one Monday morning in July. A table read -- or read-through as some call it -- is an organized reading around a table of the week's script by the actors. The Blonde was late, so we were all waiting. I might mention that we were on a sound stage, which is similar to a tin can, and since it was July, it was hot. Especially hot that particular summer. Finally, the Blonde arrives. She looks horrible. No makeup, red face, her blonde hair all askew. She looked like she had been in a fight with a bumblebee and the bee won. It was shocking. However, once she arrived the read was just getting ready to begin and the Blonde decided to give a speech. Before I go one, the back-story. There had been rumors all season about a rift between the Blonde and her co-stars. The word on the street was that the Blonde was jealous of the attention her one co-star was getting and was making the set a living hell for her. Which was true.

Now, the speech, she begins with: "I want to address you my friends and thank you for the support you have given me during this season and especially the last few weeks when lies and rumors were being thrown about and my good name being tarnished. So, thank you all. Now, I wish to speak to those enemies of mine who have been spreading these lies. Do you not realize who I am? I am world famous and have been for 25 years! I have given you a golden opportunity to work on this show and you thank me by spreading lies? How dare you! Blah, Blah, Blah, and more Blah, Blah, Blah." I'm sitting right next to the head of publicity at the studio and I punched her and said: "I think you should go lock the door to this place just in case the Blonde gets loose on the lot and bites someone!" No one said a word, and no one looked up at her. The Director said "Action" and the read began. End of back story.

Cut to a week later. I am called in to the publicity offices at the studio to discuss the fiasco of the week before at the table read. Head of publicity tells me to get *Entertainment Tonight* over there to do a 30 minute sit-down interview with our Blonde to combat and negate the rumors that our girl can't get along with her co-stars so therefore the show is being cancelled. Oh, and I was also told that I would have to convince her to participate. Whoopee!

So, first thing I do is go to Blonde's dressing room and very simply tell her that I have ET coming to the set that evening to interview her and we need her to tell them and their 30 million viewers that there is no problem at all, these are just rumors. No, she says. I had to think fast, my job and my reputation were on the line. I used the secret weapon – money.

I say, "Look, if this show is cancelled because there is trouble on the set, you would surely lose your half a million bucks you make each episode."

"Well," she says.

I continue, "And, I'll throw in one of my famous raspberry pies." That clinched it. The deal is done. On to the interview. Which, by the way went very well, and aired on *ET* that very evening. We went two more years on this show. I must have bribed her with 10 raspberry pies over the next couple of years. Out of the box? Yes, and it worked well.

More Pitching Hints to Pitch Like a Pro

1. DVR the program you want to pitch for a week.

The #1 PR complaint from TV professionals is being pitched stories and guests that don't match up with their shows' topics, format, or time slots. The harder-hitting stories typically come earlier in the broadcast and topics get fluffier as the show goes on. If you want to actually land an interview, DVR the program for a week and study it. Understand how to make a concise suggestion on where your idea fits and who would be the appropriate anchor or reporter to tell it.

2. Avoid pitching a competitor's story.

One of my dear friends who works for CNN told me of a pitch she received offering guest commentary on a developing news story that CNN was covering. The sender started the email by citing stories on the topic from other competing networks. TV producers don't want to be sent stories done by their competition, and they certainly don't want to repeat another station's story.

3. Know the shifts.

If you want to land the *Today* show, understand what time the show is on the air and don't bother to call producers then. Observe the Twitter feed of the producer with whom you are trying to connect to learn when they are clearly near their desk. Or even better, just ask when they typically have a few minutes to chat.

4. Listen for names—and use them appropriately.

One of my former co-workers has a name that can be male or female. She is female. Yet, sometimes she would receive pitches that began: "Mr. Blake." Immediate delete. Do your homework.

5. Know that the Facebook wall is off limits.

One of my friends has been pitched on his Facebook page. Aggressively calling and emailing a person to get them to hear your pitch is one thing, but don't cross the line to stalker. If you have connected on Twitter, direct messages are OK. But Facebook is different. It's personal.

And lastly, a few **common PR mistakes**.

- Don't just blast press releases. *Tell. The. Story.* A newswire spam strategy might have a temporary effect on search engine optimization, but it doesn't work long term.

- Your message has to be memorable or different or better yet, both. Not every company or product is original, but **nearly anyone can craft a distinctive, relevant story**.

- Your story doesn't spell authentic. **Authenticity is catnip**. If the customer experience doesn't live up to the claims, you'll be lucky if a lack of coverage is the result. And remember, journalists and bloggers are customers, too.

- You're drowning in **industry jargon**. Think twice before stringing together empty phrases like highly anticipated, industry leading, unique to the industry, blah, blah, blah. Just don't do it.

- Your approach is **impersonal**. The personal approach, i.e. Face Time, whether to customers or media, is crucial. PR is and always will be first and foremost about relationships.

- Your spokesperson is a **bad actor.** He or she needs to be engaged, prepared, and able to speak the speak, talk the talk, turning complicated information into easy to understand, in-layman's-terms, simple language, preferably that of the audience.

- You want a **quick fix.** You won't get one without the age-old game of **relationship building**. It is and always will be just as important in media relations as it is in sales or business development.

Is PR easy? No. Is it time-consuming and frustrating? Yes. But with the right plan, people and passion in place, you've got a good formula for building your credibility and fan base. To help you on your path, the following two chapters can help you sing like a PR canary: tools and templates and a list of business editors around the country.

Time to practice and fine-tune your performance.

CHAPTER 10
Rock star tools
TEMPLATES to go forth and rock

Like most industries, the PR and media game have certain ways of doing things and the easiest way to look like an amateur is to not follow the standard PR formats. I've included templates on how to format and present your materials so you'll pass the PR sniff test and won't embarrass yourself or your clients.

THE PRESS RELEASE – This goes out two weeks before you want it to run.

FOR IMMEDIATE RELEASE:
Contact: Name
Company
Phone
Email

Headline in TITLE CASE; Centered; Boldface; 14 Point Type
Subhead (optional); centered; 12-14 point type; bold; italics

LOS ANGELES, CA (DATE) – XYZ Company today launches its new branch of the technology giant focusing on education in technology. This is an example of a lead sentence. Remember the lead sentence should state important information about what you're announcing. The lead paragraph should state who, what, where, when and how. The entire release must be double-spaced, as it makes it easier to read.

In the second paragraph, expand on any pertinent information not included in the lead paragraph.

In the third paragraph, quote the company's founder or expert. "Avoid saying we're thrilled to announce this; rather get into the heart of why your announcement is important to your customers," says Jane Smith, CEO of XYZ Company. "For example, say that this branch of the company will strive to educate children in the Los Angeles school system."

This next paragraph is a good opportunity to list the benefits to your customer. Use bullets, it helps break up the text.

In your closing paragraph, offer additional information such as location, start date, curriculum, and anything else you need to mention.

About XYZ Company (you can single-space the boiler plate if you need to.)
This paragraph is called the boilerplate, which is a 3 - 6 sentence description of your company. Mention where your company is based, who runs it, when it was founded and what need it fills in the marketplace. End

the paragraph with your URL. For additional information, please visit www.XYZCompany.com.

# # #

3-pound signs, or hash tags, signal the end of the document.

THE MEDIA ALERT – To alert the media regarding an event you would like for them to cover. Use the who, what, when, where format. This goes out two days before the event takes place. Sample:

RELEASED FOR: Edmond Medical Center

CONTACT: Cyndy Hoenig, phone number

MEDIA ALERT!   MEDIA ALERT!   MEDIA ALERT!
For Friday, December 12, 2012

Nice Medical Center Completes Shoe Drive With ABC Elementary School

WHAT: EMC Hosts Shoe Drive for the Children at ABC Elementary School in City

WHEN: Friday, December 12
9:30 a.m. arrival at Orvis Riser

WHERE: ABC Elementary School
Street Address Here
City, State ZIP
405) 340-2984

OF NOTE: As the first adopt-a-school partnership in the city of through the Chamber of Commerce, the NMC found that many of the children at ABC come to school without shoes. A shoebox drop was put in various places at the hospital for people to donate. The hospital personnel have contributed more than 87 pairs of shoes, as well as socks, mittens, hats and coats. Delivery of these items will take place on Friday, December 12.

BIOGRAPHY – You will need bios of all key executives in your company. Following is mine in the proper format.

Biography
Cyndy Hoenig, PR Strategist

Cyndy Hoenig's career has taken her from her home in Oklahoma to a 20-year entertainment publicity career in California where she served as Director of the Consumer Television division of Bender, Goldman & Helper in Los Angeles, and back to Oklahoma. Her area of expertise centers on planning and executing media relations programs that achieve high levels of coverage. She has managed media relations for the Emmy, Screen Actors Guild and VH1 Music Awards, as well as many high profile television accounts, and for the Oklahoma City National Memorial's 10th anniversary. A program she planned and managed for Oklahoma City's Race for the Cure enhanced awareness to a level that resulted in a

35 percent increase in participation in two years.

During her career, Hoenig served as the publicist for Suzanne Somers, which included her books, TV shows, films and all ancillary items. Additionally, she is credited with launching television shows including *3rd Rock from the Sun*, *Cybill*, *The Suzanne Somers Show*, *The Five Mrs. Buchanans*, *In Living Color* and the *Mickey Mouse Club*, to name a few.

She has worked with MOW/Spelling Television, Paramount Pictures Television, Twentieth Century Fox Entertainment, The Suzanne Somers Institute., Carsey-Werner Company, CBS-Fox Video, Crown Publishing, the Disney Channel, NBC Studios, NBC Television, CBS, the WB, and Spelling Television.

Hoenig studied communications at University of Central Oklahoma and St. Edward's University in Austin, Texas. She lives in Oklahoma.

###

Fact Sheet – This is located in your media kit and on your website. It gives quick information about your company.

FACT SHEET

BUSINESS NAME
CORPORATE OVERVIEW
COMPANY HISTORY

CLIENT LIST
CERTIFICATIONS
HEADQUARTERS ADDRESS
MANAGEMENT CONTACTS
WEB SITE
MEDIA CONTACT

Backgrounder – Similar to the Fact Sheet. Goes in your media kit and on your website. The following are included in a backgrounder:

BACKGROUNDER
MISSION
HISTORY OF THE COMPANY
TOPICS / STORY IDEAS
MEDIA CONTACT

Speaking of Lingo

We PR people use a lot of lingo that I'm sure makes no sense to anyone but us. Some of our favorites include:

B-roll – "highlight" video of something we want to promote (company, person, event), often used to show broadcast outlets the potential for a story and/or provide them with footage for the story, similar to a movie trailer.

Boilerplate – short description of a company, most often used at the end of a press release.

Ed Cals – editorial calendars (predetermined story topics by media outlets).

Flack - although defined as "a publicist or promoter," it is also a derogatory reference -- often used by journalists—to describe a bad PR executive.

Hack - PR's response to "flack," often used to describe a poor journalist or reporting job.

Hits – media coverage.

In-house – a "corporate" job in which one conducts PR inside a business, as opposed to an agency job in which one services several clients at once.

Ink/Inked - signed, as in "Pure PR Inks Deal with Author Malena Lott."

Journo – a reporter (journalist).

Launch – the public marketing announcement of a people, place or product.

Opp – opportunity, as in an opportunity to get media coverage.

Pitch – note to inform/gauge interest.

Prezo – a PowerPoint presentation.

Pubs – publications, as in "we need coverage in at least 10 pubs."

Release – a news announcement.

Running/ran – article appeared.

Traction – interest/coverage.

ENCORE
Social Media Tips Too Important to keep to myself

1. **Content is King.** Content. Content. Content. Nothing is more important. You can be on all the social networks out there. But, if you are not providing interesting content, you will fail. People want to hear interesting ideas about your industry, and how-to articles or video testimonials from leaders in your field. Good content is the only way people will start feeling good about you. It is the only way you can warm up cold leads. It is through good content you will begin to convert leads to sales.

2. **Your Target Audience.** And, yes, Virginia, there is one online too. This seems obvious but so many companies are vague about who they actually want to talk to. By pinpointing your target audience, you will then be able to choose the social sites you need to be on and isolate exactly what you want to say once you get there.

3. **Show off your expertise via Social Media.** People love an expert. They buy from people who can show their expertise and one of the best things about social media is that it will make your expertise visible to the entire world. As a base, use your blog and online videos as a way to begin sharing your ideas and know-

how. Make everything your write or every video interesting, fun and thorough.

4. Social Media has a great reputation-building connection built in. And, this is why this medium goes quickly from being a friend or follower to being an absolute necessity for any serious professional.

5. Social Media is all about attitude. Social Media is far more about attitude than it is about tools. And part of that attitude means that you are ready to be open. For example, try cooperating with your competitors. Collaborate with other companies in your industry. Make your blog or website THE place to go, the most important community resource in your industry. Share your knowledge, your business tips and tricks. Open doors. Don't close them.

Social media takes time (as does PR.). You might put these tips to use and not see a return for a few months, but sooner or later, you will definitely see the benefits.

#PRTIP – Take risks. Cautiously. It gives you confidence. And there is nothing more attractive than self-confidence. Go forth and build.

PR Star Files — *And this one is about me ...*

A Publicist/PR Strategist I know used Twitter to brand herself -- successfully. A few years ago, this publicist decided to offer PR tips. She just started tweeting them about five times a day, using the hashtag #PRTips and has become known for it. It has brought approximately 15,000 followers and 4,500 Facebook friends to date. She still does it daily and says that it is the best thing she has done to brand herself. After about a year, she downloaded her tweets and put them all in an E-Book called "600 PR, Marketing & Social Media Tips to grow your business (in 140 characters or less). It is offered free on her website. So far, it's been downloaded over 50,000 times.

In conclusion, remember this: A business without a face is a business without a future. That's why it's so important for small businesses to stay visible in the ever changing and highly competitive marketplace. Staying visible requires utilizing many avenues. Too often, business owners fail to realize the importance of PR. At some point every business owner will face the challenge of promoting his products and services. PR solves this problem and doesn't cost a cent. Just start small with your community newspaper.

Chances are your first press mention won't be on the front page of *USA Today*. Start closer to home. That initial press mention in your local paper will help you establish enough credibility to approach larger media outlets. Start your press list. Journalists hate it when you pitch them something that has nothing to do with what they cover. Try mastheads.org and easymedialist.com to get this information. And, lastly, follow reporters. It's easier to craft your pitch if you know what reporters are working on. Check out editorial calendars on their websites and also at mediaontwitter.com.

About the Author

Cyndy Hoenig is a seasoned PR Professional who rose through the ranks at the prestigious Los Angeles PR firm Bender, Goldman & Helper, where she served as Director of the Consumer Television Division. Her area of expertise centers on planning and executing media relations programs that achieve high levels of coverage. She describes herself on Twitter as "a PR Strategist, Creative Writer, Gardening Addict, Proud Grandmother, Cookbook Author, True Crime Fanatic, Dog Lover & Single Girl."

Hoenig has managed campaigns for the Emmy Awards, Screen Actor's Guild, VH-1 and MTV Awards programs, as well as high-profile television programs for NBC, CBS, FOX, Aaron Spelling, Carsey-Werner, Marc Cherry & Jamie Wooten, Disney Channel, Columbia Pictures and Twentieth Television. She was the personal publicist for Suzanne Somers for more than 10 years, and has worked with Jim Carrey, Jennifer Lopez, Matthew McConaughey, Sandra Bullock and Cybill Shepherd, among many others.

In OKC, she organized the media campaign for the Oklahoma City National Memorial's Anniversary, managing the over 700 media outlets that attended. She also planned and managed a program for Oklahoma City's Race for the Cure that enhanced awareness to a level resulting in a 35% increase in participation.

Hoenig is a sustaining member of the Jr. League of

OKC and a past member of the Jr. Leagues of Austin and Los Angeles. She also serves as Communications VP for the Edmond Women's Club. Her accolades include being named a Ladies in the News Honoree by the Oklahoma Hospitality Club; receiving a Special Presidential Award from the Oklahoma Heart Association; and the Phaythopen Charity Award from the Allied Arts Foundation.

Hoenig studied communications at University of Central Oklahoma and St. Edwards University in Austin, Texas. She currently resides in Edmond, Oklahoma with her beloved Cavalier Spaniel, Digger. She has four grown daughters and eight grandchildren.

Follow me on Twitter @CyndyHoenig
Connect with me on Facebook – Cyndy
Hendrick Hoenig/Pure PR

About Pure PR

Pure PR, LLC is a full-spectrum, multi-dimensional communications firm. We bring to the table more practical, relevant experience than any other group in the state. With a proven track record of success, we have developed and implemented public relations campaigns for a wide range of companies nationwide. Our goal has always been to provide our clients with a high level of service at a reasonable cost.

We understand media and trends that influence savvy consumer customers. We have enviable relationships with national print and broadcast media. We know how to get products into the hands of those who matter, and we can craft a message and deliver it with style, so it gets noticed in a crowd.

We are seasoned professionals and our boutique size agency makes us a most effective agency. Every account is supervised by an account executive. You won't have a junior publicist cutting his teeth on your account. Our reputation attracts both large companies and young, entrepreneurial start-ups.

Our clients are our biggest fans. They refer new business to us and hire us again and again. Our proven track record shows how relentless we are when it comes to securing key press, creating brand identity with media and consumers, positioning products and services as must-haves, influencing the influential, and providing unmatched client service.

When you work with Pure PR, you'll see results.

We deliver on our promise to build press campaigns that get our clients featured in top-tier print, broadcast and Internet outlets. We'll help you secure media coverage that creates and builds name recognition and buzz, establishes credibility, and ultimately increases your business potential.

Encore two
VIPs: top 100 newspaper business editors

Start your PR Engines. Below are the top 100 business editors so you can start your media list. Be sure and check the website and/or call the outlet to ensure the person is still in that position before you pitch them. (2/1/13)

Akron Beacon Journal
Larry Pantages
Lpantages
@thebeaconjournal.com
330.996.3000
330.996.3033
PO Box 640
Akron OH 44309-0640

Albany Times Union
Eric Anderson
eanderson@timesunion.com
518.454.5694
518.454.5628
Box 15000
Albany NY 12212

Albuquerque Journal
Michael Murphy
mmurphy@abqjournal.com
505.823.3800
505.823.3994
7777 Jefferson Street NE
Albuquerque NM 87109

Allentown Morning Call
Christine Schiavo
christine.schiavo@mcall.com
610.820.6500
610.820.6693
101 North Sixth Street
Allentown PA 18101

Arizona Daily Star
Norma Coile
business@azstarnet.com
800.695.4492
520.573.4200
4850 S. Park Ave.
Tucson AZ 85714

Arizona Republic
Kathy Tulumello
kathy.tulumello@arizonarep-ublic.com
602.444.8000
602.444.8933
PO Box 1950
Phoenix AZ 85001

Arkansas Democrat-Gazette
Jack Weatherly
jweatherly@arkansasonline.com
501.378.3400

501.372.4765
PO Box 2221
Little Rock AR 72203

Arlington Heights Daily Herald
Lisa Miner
lminer@dailyherald.com
847.427.4300
847.427.1301
PO Box 280
Arlington Heights IL 60006-0280

Asbury Park Press
Dennis Carmody
business@app.com
732.922.6000
732.643.4014
3601 Hwy 66
Neptune NJ 07754

Atlanta Journal-Constitution
Matt Kempner
mkempner@ajc.com
404.526.5151
404.526.5746
223 Perimeter Center Pkwy.
Atlanta GA 30346

Austin American-Statesman
Kathy Warbelow
business@statesman.com
512.445.3500
Not accepted
PO Box 670
Austin TX 78767

Baltimore Sun
Liz Hacken
businessnews@baltsun.com
410.332.6000
410.332.6455
501 N. Calvert St.
Baltimore MD 21278

Baton Rouge Advocate
Bobby Lamb
blamb@theadvocate.com
225.383.1111
225.388.0175
PO Box 588
Baton Rouge LA 70821-0588

Bergen County Record
Bill Donnellon
donnellon@northjersey.com
973.569.7000
201.457.2520
PO Box 471
Woodland Park NJ 07424

Birmingham News
Jerry Underwood
biznews@bhamnews.com
205.325.4444
205.325.3345
PO Box 2553
Birmingham AL 35202

Boston Globe
Shirley Leung
sleung@globe.com
617.929.2000
617.929.2098
PO Box 55819
Boston MA 02205-5819

Boston Herald
Frank Quaratiello
business@bostonherald.com
617.426.3000
617.619.6450
70 Fargo Street

Boston MA 02110

Buffalo News
Grove Potter
gpotter@buffnews.com
716.849.4444
716.856.5150
PO Box 100
Buffalo NY 14240

Charleston Post and Courier
John McDermott
jmcdermott@postandcourier.com
843.577.7111
843.937.5579
134 Columbus Street
Charleston SC 29403

Charlotte Observer
Patrick Scott
obsbiz@charlotteobserver.com
704.358.5000
704.358.5036
600 S. Tryon St.
Charlotte NC 28202

Chattanooga Times Free Press
John Vass
jvass@timesfreepress.com
423.756.6900
423.757.6520
400 East 11th St.
Chattanooga TN 37403

Chicago Sun-Times
Polly Smith
psmith@suntimes.com
312.321.3000
312.321.2120
350 N. Orleans St.
10th Floor
Chicago IL 60654

Chicago Tribune
Michael Lev
mlev@tribune.com
312.222.3232
435 N. Michigan Avenue
Chicago IL 60611

Cincinnati Enquirer
Lee Ann Hamilton
business@enquirer.com
513.768.8000
513.768.8340
312 Elm St.
Cincinnati OH 45202

Cleveland Plain Dealer
Randy Roguski
rroguski@plaind.com
216.999.4800
216.999.6374
1801 Superior Avenue
Cleveland OH 44114

Colorado Springs Gazette
Bill Radford
businessnews@gazette.com
719.632.5511
719.636.0202
30 S. Prospect St.
Colorado Springs CO 80903

Columbus Dispatch
Ron Carter
rcarter@dispatch.com
614.461.5000
614.461.7580
34 S. 3rd St.
Columbus OH 43215

Contra Costa Times
Steve Trousdale
strousdale@bayareanewsgroup.com

925.935.2525
925.943.8362
2640 Shadelands Drive
Walnut Creek CA 94598

Dallas Morning News
Dennis Fulton
businessnews@dallasnews.com
214.977.8222
214.977.8319
508 Young Street
Dallas TX 75202

Dayton Daily News
Mary Irby-Jones
mirby@daytondailynews.com
937.225.2000
937.225.2489
1611 S. Main St.
Dayton OH 45409

Daytona Beach News-Journal
Clayton Park
clayton.park@news-jrnl.com
386.252.1511
386.258.8465
901 Sixth Street
Daytona Beach FL 32117

Delaware News Journal
Doug Williams
dwilliams@delawareonline.com
302.324.2500
302.324.5509
PO Box 15505
Wilmington DE 19850

Denver Post
Kristi Arellano
business@denverpost.com
303.954.1010
303.954.1369
101 W. Colfax Ave.
Suite 600
Denver CO 80202-5177

Des Moines Register
Lynn Hicks
lhicks@dmreg.com
515.284.8000
515.286.2504
PO Box 957
Des Moines IA 50304-0957

Detroit Free Press
Sarah Webster
swebster@freepress.com
313.222.6400
313.222.5981
615 W. Lafayette Blvd.
Detroit MI 48226

Detroit News
Joanna Firestone
jfirestone@detnews.com
313.222.2300
313.496.5400
615 W. Lafayette Blvd.
Detroit MI 48226

El Paso Times
Paula Diaz
pdiaz@elpasotimes.com
915.546.6100
915.546.6415
300 N. Campbell St.
El Paso TX 79901

Florida Times-Union
Wayne Ezell
wayne.ezell@jacksonville.com
904.359.4111
904.359.4478
PO Box 1949
Jacksonville FL 32231

Fort Worth Star-Telegram
Jim Fuquay
jfuquay@star-telegram.com
817.390.7761
817.390.7789
PO Box 1870
Fort Worth TX 76101

Fresno Bee
Robert Zizzo
business@fresnobee.com
559.441.6111
559.441.6436
1626 E Street
Fresno CA 93786

Harrisburg Patriot-News
Jack Sherzer
jsherzer@patriot-news.com
717.255.8100
717.255.8456
2020 Technology Parkway
Suite 300
Mechanicsburg PA 17050

Hartford Courant
Dan Haar
dhaar@courant.com
860.241.6200
860.520.6941
285 Broad St.
Hartford CT 06115

Honolulu Star-Advertiser
David Butts
dbutts@staradvertiser.com
808.529.4700
808.529.4750
500 Ala Moana #7-210
Honolulu HI 96813

Houston Chronicle
Laura Goldberg
laura.goldberg@chron.com
713.362.7171
713.362.6806
PO Box 4260
Houston TX 77210-4260

Indianapolis Star
Greg Weaver
greg.weaver@indystar.com
317.444.4444
317.444.6600
PO Box 145
Indianapolis IN 46206-0145

Intelligencer Journal-Lancaster New Era
Tim Mekeel
business@lnpnews.com
717.291.8811
717.399.6507
PO Box 1328
Lancaster PA 17608

Investor's Business Daily
Ken Popovich
ken.popovich@investors.com
310.448.6700
310.577.7350
12655 Beatrice Street
Los Angeles CA 90066

Kansas City Star
Keith Chrostowski
chrostowski@kcstar.com
816.234.4636
1729 Grand Blvd.
Kansas City MO 64108

Knoxville News Sentinel
Bill Brewer
biznews@knoxnews.com
865.521.8181
865.342.6400
2332 News Sentinel Drive

Knoxville TN 37921

La Opinion
Pedro Rojas
pedro.rojas@laopinion.com
213.622.8332
213.896.2171
700 S. Flower Street
Suite 700
Los Angeles CA 90017

Las Vegas Review-Journal
James Wright
jwright@reviewjournal.com
702.383.0211
702.383.4676
PO Box 70
Las Vegas NV 89125

Lexington Herald-Leader
Tom Caudill
tcaudill@herald-leader.com
859.231.3100
859.231.3224
100 Midland Avenue
Lexington KY 40508-1999

Lincoln Journal Star
Dick Piersol
dpiersol@journalstar.com
402.475.4200
402.473.7291
926 P Street
Lincoln NE 68508

Long Beach Press-Telegram
Kristopher Hanson
kristopher.hanson@presstelegram.com
562.435.1161
562.499.1277
300 Oceangate
Long Beach CA 90844

Los Angeles Daily News
Barbara Jones
barbara.jones@dailynews.com
818.713.3000
818.713.0058
PO Box 4200
Woodland Hills CA 91367

Los Angeles Times
John Corrigan
business@latimes.com
213.237.5000
213.237.4712
202 W. 1st Street
Los Angeles CA 90012

Louisville Courier-Journal
Dan Blake
dblake@courier-journal.com
502.582.4711
502.582.4200
PO Box 740031
Louisville KY 40201-7431

Memphis Commercial Appeal
Roland Klose
klose@commercialappeal.com
901.529.2345
901.529.6476
495 Union Avenue
Memphis TN 38103

Miami Herald
Jane Wooldridge
business@MiamiHerald.com
305.350.2111
305.376.8950
One Herald Plaza
Miami FL 33132

Milwaukee Journal Sentinel
Chuck Melvin
cmelvin@journalsentinel.com
414.224.2000

414.224.2047
PO Box 371
Milwaukee WI 53201

Mobile Press-Register
K.A. Turner
kturner@press-register.com
251.219.5400
251.219.5794
PO Box 2488
Mobile AL 36652-2488

Nashville Tennessean
Deborah Fisher
dfisher@tennessean.com
615.259.8000
615.259.8093
1100 Broadway
Nashville TN 37203

New Haven Register
Cara Baruzzi
cbaruzzi@nhregister.com
203.789.5200
203.865.7894
40 Sargent Drive
New Haven CT 06511

New Orleans Times-Picayune
Kim Quillen
money@timespicayune.com
504.826.3279
504.826.3812
3800 Howard Avenue
New Orleans LA 70125-1429

New York Daily News
Robert Dominguez
rdominguez@nydailynews.com
212.210.2100
212.643.7831
4 New York Plaza
New York NY 10004

New York Post
Dan Greenfield
dgreenfield@nypost.com
212.930.8000
212.930.8540
1211 Avenue of the Americas
New York NY 10036-8790

New York Times
Larry Ingrassia
bizday@nytimes.com
212.556.1234
646.428.6227
620 8th Avenue
New York NY 10018

Newark Star-Ledger
Rick Everett
business@starledger.com
973.392.4040
973.392.5845
1 Star-Ledger Plaza
Newark NJ 07102

Newport News Daily Press
Dave Hendrickson
dhendrickson@dailypress.com
757.247.4600
757.247.4848
7505 Warwick Blvd.
Newport News VA 23607

Newsday
Bob McGough
bob.mcgough@newsday.com
800.639.7329
631.843.2375
235 Pinelawn Rd.
Melville NY 11747

North County Times
Dan McSwain

dmcswain@nctimes.com
760.745.6611
760.745.3769
207 E. Pennsylvania Ave.
Escondido CA 92025

Northwest Indiana Times
Matt Saltanovitz
msaltanovitz@nwitimes.com
219.933.3200
219.933.3249
601 W. 45th Ave.
Munster IN 46321

Oakland Press
Joseph Szczesny
joe.szczesny@oakpress.com
248.332.8181
48 West Huron
Pontiac MI 48342

Oklahoman
Clytie Bunyan
cbunyan@opubco.com
405.475.3311
405.475.3183
PO Box 25125
Oklahoma City OK 73125

Omaha World-Herald
Deb Shanahan
Deb.Shanahan@owh.com
402.444.1000
402.444.1231
1314 Douglas Street
Suite 100
Omaha NE 68102

Orange County Register
Julie Gallego
business@ocregister.com
877.469.7344
625 N. Grand Ave.
Santa Ana CA 92701

Orlando Sentinel
Lisa Cianci
businessnews@orlandosentinel.com
407.420.5000
407.420.5350
633 N. Orange Ave.
Orlando FL 32801

Palm Beach Post
Carolyn DiPaolo
pbbusiness@pbpost.com
561.820.4400
561.820.4407
PO Box 24700
West Palm Beach FL 33416

Philadelphia Daily News
Wendy Warren
wwarren@phillynews.com
215.854.5901
215.854.5910
400 N. Broad St.
Philadelphia PA 19130

Philadelphia Inquirer
Brian Toolan
btoolan@phillynews.com
215.854.4500
215.854.5099
400 N. Broad St.
Philadelphia PA 19130

Pittsburgh Post-Gazette
Brian Hyslop
bhyslop@post-gazette.com
412.263.1100
412.391.8452
34 Blvd. of the Allies
Pittsburgh PA 15222

Pittsburgh Tribune-Review
John Oravecz
business@tribweb.com

412.321.6460
412.320.7965
503 Martindale Street
3rd Floor
Pittsburgh PA 15212

Portland Oregonian
Scott Bernard Nelson
Money@oregonian.com
503.221.8327
503.227.5306
1320 SW Broadway
Portland OR 97201

Providence Journal
John Kostrzewa
jkostrze@projo.com
401.277.7000
401.277.7346
75 Fountain Street
Providence RI 02902

Raleigh News & Observer
Mary Cornatzer
mary.cornatzer@newsobserver.com
919.829.4500
919.829.4872
PO Box 191
Raleigh NC 27602

Richmond Times-Dispatch
John Hoke
jhoke@timesdispatch.com
804.649.6000
804.775.8059
Box 85333
Richmond VA 23293

Riverside Press-Enterprise
Mark Coast
mcoast@pe.com
951.684.1200
951.368.9023
3450 Fourteenth Street
Riverside CA 92501

Roanoke Times
Brian Kelley
brian.kelley@roanoke.com
540.981.3211
540.981.3346
PO Box 2491
Roanoke VA 24010-2491

Rochester Democrat and Chronicle
Steve Sink
ssink@democratandchronicle.com
585.232.7100
585.258.2485
55 Exchange Blvd.
Rochester NY 14614

Sacramento Bee
Mary Lynne Vellinga
mlvellinga@sacbee.com
916.321.1000
916.321.1109
PO Box 15779
Sacramento CA 95852

Salt Lake Tribune
Michael Limon
mlimon@sltrib.com
801.257.8742
801.257.8525
90 S. 400 West
Suite 700
Salt Lake City UT 84101

San Antonio Express-News
Emily Spicer
espicer@express-news.net
210.250.3000

210.250.3105
PO Box 2171
San Antonio TX 78297-2171

San Diego Union-Tribune
Diana McCabe
diana.mccabe@uniontrib.com
800.533.8830
619.293.1896
PO Box 120191
San Diego CA 92112-0191

San Francisco Chronicle
Kevin Keane
kkeane@sfchronicle.com
415.777.1111
415.896.1107
901 Mission Street
San Francisco CA 94103

San Jose Mercury News
Steve Trousdale
business@mercurynews.com
408.920.5000
408.288.8060
750 Ridder Park Drive
San Jose CA 95190

Sarasota Herald-Tribune
Matthew Sauer
matthew.sauer@heraldtribune.com
941.953.7755
1741 Main St
Sarasota FL 34236

Seattle Times
Becky Bisbee
business@seattletimes.com
206.464.2111
206.464.2261
PO Box 70
Seattle WA 98111

South Carolina State
Andy Shane
biznews@thestate.com
803.771.6161
803.771.8430
PO Box 1333
Columbia SC 29202

South Florida Sun-Sentinel
Cyndi Metzger
CMetzger@sun-sentinel.com
954.356.4000
954.356.4559
500 E. Broward Blvd
Fort Lauderdale FL 33394

Spokane Spokesman-Review
Scott Maben
scottm@spokesman.com
509.459.5000
509.459.5482
PO Box 2160
Spokane WA 99210

St. Louis Post-Dispatch
Irvin Harrell
iharrell@post-dispatch.com
314.340.8000
314.340.3050
900 North Tucker Blvd.
St. Louis MO 63101

St. Paul Pioneer Press
Chris Clonts
cclonts@pioneerpress.com
651.222.1111
651.228.5564
345 Cedar Street
St. Paul MN 55101

St. Petersburg Times
Bob Trigaux
biznews@sptimes.com
727.893.8111

727.893.8675
490 First Avenue South
St. Petersburg FL 33701

Tampa Tribune
Mark Guidera
mguidera@tampatrib.com
813.259.7600
813.259.8080
200-202 S. Parker Street
Tampa FL 33606

Toledo Blade
Greg Braknis
gbraknis@theblade.com
419.724.6000
419.724.6439
541 N. Superior St.
Toledo OH 43660

Torrance Daily Breeze
Muhammed El-Hasan
muhammed.elhasan@dailybreeze.com
310.540.5511
21250 Hawthorne Blvd.
Suite 170
Torrance CA 90503

Tulsa World
John Stancavage
john.stancavage@tulsaworld.com
918.581.8400
918.581.8353
315 S. Boulder Ave.
Tulsa OK 74103

USA Today
Doug Caroll
dcarroll@usatoday.com
703.854.3400
703.854.2165
7950 Jones Branch Drive
McLean VA 22108-0605

Ventura County Star
Ken Maryanski
kmaryanski@vcstar.com
805.437.0000
805.482.6167
PO Box 6006
Camarillo CA 93011

Virginian-Pilot
Chris Dinsmore
chris.dinsmore@pilotonline.com
757.446.2000
757.446.2414
150 Brambleton Ave.
Norfolk VA 23501-0449

Wall Street Journal
Alan Murray
nywireroom@dowjones.com
212.416.2000
1211 Avenue of the Americas
New York NY 10036

Washington Post
Dan Beyers
beyersd@washpost.com
202.334.6000
1150 15th Street NW
Washington DC 20071

Wichita Eagle
Tom Shine
tshine@wichitaeagle.com
316.268.6000
316.269.6799
825 E. Douglas
Wichita KS 67202

Wisconsin State Journal (WSJ)
Thomas Enwright
tenwright@madison.com
608.252.6100

608.252.6119
PO Box 8056
Madison WI 53708

Worcester Telegram & Gazette
Bob Kievra
rkievra@telegram.com
508.793.9100
508.793.9313
PO Box 15012
Worcester MA 01615-0012

What are you waiting for?
Your audience awaits.

Also in the **Little Brand** Series:

The Little Brand That Could by Malena Lott coming Spring 2013.

For more titles by Buzz Books, visit www.buzzbooksusa.com.

2013 Titles include:
TMI Mom: Oversharing My Life by Heather Davis (humorous essays)
Dance Mom Survival Guide by Malena Lott and Jill Martin (dance, parenting)
Mark of the Centipede Timeshifters Book 1 by Cara Brookins (Young adult novel)
Family Charms by Malena Lott (mainstream fiction)
Twin Falls Book 1 by Lena Brown (Young adult novel)
Chicago Fell First by Aaron Smith (Horror novel)

www.ingramcontent.com/pod-product-compliance
Lightning Source LLC
Chambersburg PA
CBHW030003050426
42451CB00006B/94